How Many Muscles Make Your Smile?

Questions About Muscles and Movement

by **Thomas Canavan**

PowerKiDS press™

Published in 2017 by **The Rosen Publishing Group, Inc.**
29 East 21st Street, New York, NY 10010

Cataloging-in-Publication Data
Names: Canavan, Thomas.
Title: How many muscles make your smile? / Thomas Canavan.
Description: New York : PowerKids Press, 2017. | Series: Human body FAQ | Includes index.
Identifiers: ISBN 9781499431667 (pbk.) | ISBN 9781499432237 (library bound) |
  ISBN 9781499431674 (6 pack)
Subjects: LCSH: Musculoskeletal system--Juvenile literature. | Muscles--Juvenile literature.
Classification: LCC QP301.C317 2017 | DDC 612.7--dc23

Author: Thomas Canavan
Designers: Supriya Sahai and Emma Randall
Editors: Joe Harris and Anna Brett

Picture credits: Cover illustration: Shutterstock. Interior illustrations: Shutterstock

Manufactured in the United States of America
CPSIA Compliance Information: Batch #BW17PK: For Further Information contact Rosen Publishing, New York, New York at 1-800-237-9932.

Contents

Why do we need muscles?

We need muscles to perform just about any activity that involves movement. These bundles of fibrous (stringy) tissues do so many things. They move your bones, open your eyes, and help you chew. Many of them work automatically, pumping your heart, helping you digest food, and making sure you breathe regularly.

Why can you hear your heart?

Each thump of your heartbeat is the sound of a heart muscle forcing a heart valve (part of the heart that controls the flow of blood) shut.

Which muscles make you talk?

Your tongue, a collection of muscles, forms many sounds. Even opening and closing your mouth to form other sounds depends on muscles in your face and jaw. And in order to force the air out of your mouth to make a sound, you need to use the diaphragm muscle below your lungs.

How are we moving when we're keeping still?

Imagine that your body is a factory. It may look calm and quiet outside, but inside there is lots going on. Goods are being moved around, doors are opening and closing, and fuel is powering all of the machines. Your muscles keep your body "factory" up and running, even if you're not moving around.

What do muscles look like?

If you looked closely at an elastic band, you'd see that it is made up of strands that stretch and then tighten up again. Close up, muscles look a lot like that, but they have special shapes to match their job. All of them respond to signals from your brain, telling them to contract (tighten) or relax.

Do your eyes really have muscles?

Yes! The iris has a muscle that opens and closes the pupil to control incoming light, and there are six muscles around your eye that move your eyeball.

How many muscles are there in your body?

Your body has about 640 muscles. Some people consider some of those to be groups of smaller muscles, so the total could be much higher. Whatever the number, they make up three main groups: skeletal (which move bones), cardiac (in your heart), and smooth (mainly in your digestive system).

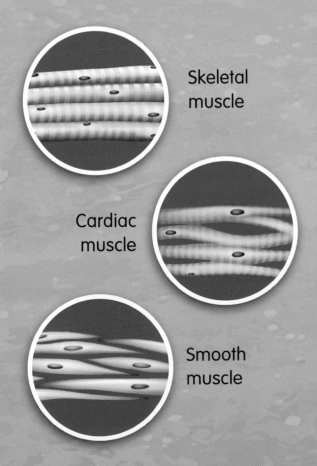

Skeletal muscle

Cardiac muscle

Smooth muscle

What are different muscles like?

Skeletal muscles are made of light and dark bands called fibrils, making them looked striped. They are the only muscles that we control, and most are connected to bones. Cardiac muscles, which pump blood in and out of the heart, are also made up of shaded bands. The smooth muscles on the walls of many internal organs get their name because they lack stripes.

Which muscle is the most important?

The heart contains the most important muscles in your body. Without them you wouldn't be alive! These muscles make the heart beat about 100,000 times a day and they do the most work of any muscles during a lifetime. The stronger your heart muscles are, the better your body can function.

How big is your heart?
Lock your hands together with the fingers entwined. That's about the size of your heart.

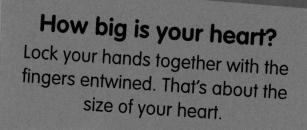

How do you measure the strength of your heart?

An electrocardiogram (ECG) machine measures the electricity going through the heart with every beat the muscles make. But an easier way to measure your heart rate is to take your pulse. How many times does your heart beat in a minute?

How does your heart keep in rhythm?

The outer walls of your heart contain a group of muscle cells that produce a small electrical current. These electrical pulses make your heart beat at a safe, steady pace.

Which muscle is the smallest?

The stapedius muscle in your middle ear is less than 0.08 inch (2 mm) long. It controls the vibration of the smallest bone in your body, the stapes, which in turn protects your inner ear from high noise levels.

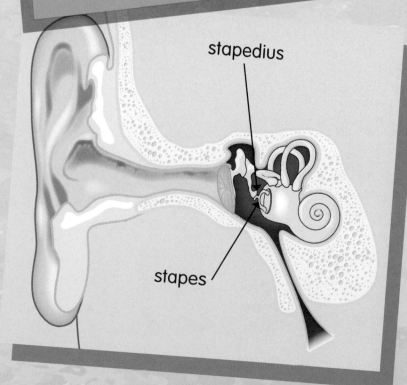

stapedius

stapes

How do muscles help us move?

Skeletal muscles help you move around. They are connected to bones with tough tissues called tendons and work by pulling rather than pushing. As a muscle contracts, it pulls a tendon connected to a bone. That pulls the bone with it. You're in control of these muscles, which tighten or relax as you instruct them.

How many muscles does it take to walk?

The simple act of taking a step involves several movements. You need to lift one leg off the floor, move it forward, place it back down, and keep your balance at the same time. This uses muscles in your hips, bottom, thighs, lower leg, feet, toes, and also your arms, waist, tummy, and back. At a rough count, it's around 200 muscles!

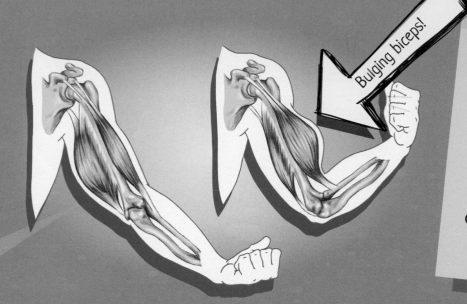

Bulging biceps!

Why do muscles work in pairs?

Muscles often pair up on each side of a bone or joint. When you bend your arm, you're tightening the biceps muscle on one side of your upper arm. At the same time, you're relaxing the triceps muscle underneath. To straighten out again you just do the opposite with the pair.

Which is your largest muscle?
The largest muscles in your body are the gluteus maximus muscles in your bottom. They move your back and your largest bone, the femur (thigh bone).

CRE-E-E-A-K!!

Can muscles really remember?

It's true that muscles can seem to remember a series of movements in the right order. It's called muscle memory. But in reality, it's your brain that's calling the shots. Like a computer with a set of stored commands, your brain stores a series of signals that it sends out to muscles when certain actions are needed.

Does practice always make perfect?

Unfortunately, muscle memory doesn't necessarily make you do things better. It can also stop you from improving, if you keep making the same mistakes.

12

Why do we need muscle memory?

Imagine having to think about every movement of your arm whenever you served a tennis ball, or every single twist of your fingers when you tie your shoes. Luckily your muscles can be trained to do repeated actions the same way again and again.

Can it help you play the piano?

Yes, as long as you learn the correct notes. Age is no barrier to muscle memory—Jacob Velazquez from Florida could play entire works by Beethoven when he was five.

Can artificial muscles develop a memory?

Many artificial limbs combine smooth movement with comfort, but until recently, the "muscles" in these limbs couldn't perform repeated actions as quickly as human muscles. Scientists have now developed ways of chemically recording the movements of artificial limbs so that they can perform patterns of movement quickly, just like human muscles.

Can muscles work by themselves?

Your body never shuts off. It's working 24/7, even if you're asleep. Muscles provide the movement and activity to keep things running. Involuntary, or smooth, muscles line the walls of organs and blood vessels. Their contractions help move blood, food, and other substances through the body.

Can your muscles turn you into a caveman?

When you're suddenly scared, your brain sends a signal to glands that produce a chemical called epinephrine (or adrenaline). Your heart rate speeds up and blood rushes to your muscles, ready for you to fight anything dangerous— or run away from it, just as early humans would once have done when under attack.

Aarrghh!

Can heart muscles mix up signals?

Yes, they can. Some people can have an irregular heartbeat treated with a device called a pacemaker, which sends out regular pulses to the cardiac muscles.

Why do we breathe faster sometimes?

Your diaphragm muscle controls your breathing. The speed it works at depends on how much carbon dioxide (a waste product) is in your blood. If there's a lot, like when you exercise, then you breathe fast. If levels are low, like when you're asleep, then your brain tells your diaphragm to make you breathe more slowly. It's automatic.

How do muscles build up?

If you and a weight lifter stood next to each other and flexed your muscles, the weight lifter's muscles would look much bigger than yours. Weight lifters build up their muscles by lifting heavy loads. But it's more important that you keep your muscles strong with regular exercise than focus on bodybuilding!

Do all exercises build up muscles?

Different forms of exercise help keep muscles strong, but some weight lifting causes tiny rips in the muscles. Those muscles get a little bigger (or bulk up) as they heal.

Can you lengthen your muscles?

It's impossible to lengthen your muscles, because they are attached to tendons and bones at each end. They grow when you're young but stop when you reach adult height. Imagine a road linking two cities. You couldn't lengthen that road, but you could widen it. Bulking out muscles widens them.

What are your core muscles?

It's not only your arms and legs that use muscles. Your central body has muscles that are extremely important for all-around movement. The muscles in your stomach (your "abs" or "six-pack") and lower back keep you strong and help you sit up straighter, walk better, and feel good if they are toned.

What is a muscle cramp?

Chemicals are exchanged each time muscles contract and relax. The tissues in a resting muscle are long and stretched. When the tissues tighten and the muscle contracts, calcium rushes in and sodium (salt) goes out. Normally the muscle relaxes again quickly, but sometimes it stays tightly and painfully constricted. That's a muscle cramp.

What causes a cramp in your side?

The sharp pain in your side when you exercise is thought to be a cramp in the diaphragm. Stretch to the opposite side from the stitch to relieve it.

Does exercise after eating cause cramps?

Probably not, but you are likely to feel sick or sluggish if you exercise too soon after eating. During exercise, your blood flow is diverted to your muscles from your digestive system. This can make it harder to deal with large amounts of food.

Do muscles ever move by mistake?

Involuntary muscle movements (called tics or twitches) are usually temporary and caused when nerve endings accidentally fire a signal to a muscle.

Glug glug!!

Are cramps bad for you?

Most cramps are harmless results of exercising too much or too fast, or not drinking enough water beforehand. That makes it harder for muscles to receive and get rid of nutrients or waste. However, very severe, prolonged, or frequent cramps could be signs of bigger medical problems.

Do muscles need special fuel?

Muscles get most of their energy from glucose, a type of sugar that is found in many foods. They use oxygen contained in the blood to convert the glucose into energy. This is a chemical reaction, and it also releases water and carbon dioxide. The energy can be used right away or stored as fuel for later.

Why do tennis players eat bananas?

Bananas contain lots of carbohydrates (which release glucose) as well as potassium, which helps prevent cramps.

ACE!

Does a balanced diet help muscles?

A balanced diet usually refers to eating a sensible mixture of foods providing protein, fat, and carbohydrates. That balance helps most of your body's systems, and is especially good for muscles. Carbohydrates such as potatoes, pasta, and grains provide energy. Fat stores some of that energy, and protein is the "building block" of muscles.

Is losing weight bad for your muscles?

Yes, because if people try to lose weight too fast, their bodies might use muscles, rather than fat, as a source of energy.

Are energy drinks helpful?

Energy drinks promise to promote strength and alertness, but often rely on lots of sugar (to provide glucose) and caffeine (the drug in coffee that keeps people awake). You shouldn't have too much of either of these. Instead, eat a banana for energy, drink water to stop dehydration, and have a glass of chocolate milk after doing sports; it provides a great mix of nutrients for your muscles. Yummy!

Why does exercise "burn" sometimes?

Have you heard people talk about "feeling the burn" when their muscles are working hard? That's because oxygen in your blood helps your muscles use glucose to produce energy. If you're exercising really hard, then the muscles use up all the oxygen in the blood nearby. The muscles now start to turn sugar into oxygen. Lactic acid is left behind, giving your muscles a burning feeling.

Does exercise make you happy?

Scientists have found that muscles that work hard produce chemicals called endorphins, which send "I feel happy" signals to the brain.

Can we exercise too much?

Feeling the burn is a sign that your muscles have been working hard. That can be a good thing, but it's also one of the signals that things have gone too far and that you need rest. If too much lactic acid is left behind, then your muscles can be damaged.

How much exercise do you need?

Young people should try to do one hour every day. It doesn't matter what form the exercise takes, as long as it makes you breathe faster and sweat a little. It can be dancing, swimming, skateboarding, playing ball games, climbing trees, martial arts, riding your bike, or running around the block with your dog.

Do older people need to exercise?

Some muscle turns to fat as people get older, so it's important to exercise regularly to keep those muscle levels maintained.

How do muscles keep us warm?

As well as "feeling the burn" and "burning calories," muscles really can produce heat, and help you to keep warm when the outside temperature starts to fall. Calories measure a form of heat linked to energy. That energy provides fuel for your muscles to act like a central heating system.

What happens when we shiver?

Your body can sense when cold is a threat. The brain sends signals to muscles on your skin, making them contract and relax very quickly. As they do so, they release heat.

Can muscles shrink?

If muscles aren't used enough, they become small and weak. Astronauts use less muscle in space because they aren't working against gravity the whole time. To make up for this they have to exercise every day. On the International Space Station, astronauts spend over two hours per day working out.

Phew!

What causes goose bumps?

Muscles cause tiny hairs on your body to stand up, pulling skin up in bumps. The standing hairs trap warm air to act as a blanket against the cold. The scientific name is horripilation!

Why do athletes warm up before performing?

Warming up is a slow-motion way to prepare your muscles for activity. It helps loosen the muscles, making exercise easier, and it increases your heart and breathing rates to send more blood and oxygen to muscles. Plus, it really does warm up muscles, and warmer muscles can get oxygen from the blood faster.

Can muscles get sick?

Normal biceps

Biceps with muscular dystrophy

Muscular dystrophy is a genetic disease that damages muscle fibers and causes them to weaken and waste away. This can cause pain, weakness and even paralysis. Keeping active and stretching regularly can help affected people to stay mobile for longer as this increases blood flow to the muscles.

How many muscles make your smile?

People use many combinations of muscles to make a variety of smiles: between ten and 43 muscles for any smile.

How much of the body is made of muscle?

Around 40% of your total body weight is muscle. The rest of your body weight is made up of your organs, bones, and everything else inside you.

How many muscles make your frown?

People commonly say it takes more muscles to frown than to smile, but there isn't a straightforward answer… because there are so many types of smiles and frowns. However, smiling makes you feel better, so work those multiple muscles!

Why are some runners better at endurance than others?

There are two types of skeletal muscles, fast twitch and slow twitch. Slow twitch muscle fibers contract slowly but can keep working for a long time. Fast twitch fibers contract quickly but get tired just as fast. Champion sprinters have more fast twitch muscles than most and vice versa for long-distance runners.

27

How does everything work together?

Our bodies are made up of different systems. Each system has its own function, such as converting food into energy, or removing waste. The systems all work together to bring the human body to life.

Circulatory system

Your heart is at the center of this system, which pumps blood around your body via veins and arteries.

Skeletal system

All 206 bones make up the skeletal system, which supports and protects your body.

Muscular system

Around 640 muscles in your body help you move. Your muscles are attached to your bones by tendons.

Respiratory system

Your lungs draw in air to bring oxygen into the body and push air out to move carbon dioxide out.

Nervous system

The brain passes messages around the body via a system of nerves. Nerves also pass messages received by your senses back to the brain.

Excretory system

Toxins and waste materials are removed from your body by this system, which includes your kidneys and bladder.

Digestive system

This system takes in food, and breaks it down into energy and basic nutrients the body can use.

Endocrine system

Glands in this system produce chemicals called hormones that help you grow and change your mood.

Testes (male)

Ovaries (female)

Glossary

alert Able to think clearly and notice things around you.

artificial Not natural, but made to work like something that is.

calorie A unit for measuring the energy contained in food.

carbohydrate A type of sugar made by plants that the body uses to produce and store energy.

carbon dioxide A colorless, odorless gas produced when the human body respires and breathes out.

cardiac muscles Muscles in the heart.

contract A movement that makes something smaller or shorter.

diaphragm The muscle beneath the lungs that controls breathing.

endurance The ability to do something for a long time.

energy The power to be active and perform jobs.

fat A chemical substance that the body produces to store energy. It is stored in fat cells beneath the skin or surrounding organs.

fibrous Made of fibers.

gravity A natural force on Earth that causes things to move towards each other.

involuntary muscles The muscles that work without any conscious control, for example the muscles that keep your heart beating.

iris The colored part of the eye that opens and closes to control the amount of light entering the eye.

nerves Fibers in the body that transmit messages around the body.

nutrient A substance that the body needs for energy or growth.

oxygen A colorless, odorless gas found in the air that the body breathes in.

protein One of the most important of all molecules in the body, protein is needed to strengthen and replace tissue in the body.

pulse The regular beat felt in the wrist or the neck as the heart pumps blood around the body.

relax To cause something to become less tight or stiff.

skeletal muscles Muscles that are attached to your bones.

smooth muscles Muscles found in hollow organs such as blood vessels, the intestines, and the bladder.

tendon A tough tissue that connects a muscle to a bone.

toned Strong and firm.

valve A structure that allows fluid to move in one direction only by stopping it from flowing backwards.

Further Information

Further reading

Complete Book of the Human Body *by Anna Claybourne*
(Usborne Books, 2013)

How Your Body Works: Moving Your Body *by Philip Morgan*
(Franklin Watts, 2011)

Human Body: A Children's Encyclopedia *by editors of DK*
(Dorling Kindersley, 2012)

Human Body Factory *by Dan Green* (Kingfisher, 2012)

Human Body: Fascinating Facts *by editors at Collins* (Collins, 2016)

Make and Move: Human Body *by Anita Ganeri* (Silver Dolphin Books, 2016)

Websites

PowerKids Press has developed an online list of websites related to the subject of this book. This site is updated regularly. Please use this link to access the list: **www.powerkidslinks.com/hbfaq/muscles**

Index